11 o'clock
12 o'clock
1 o'clock
5 o'clock
6 o'clock
7 o'clock

Parents are often surprised by the quality and depth of their child's memory and observation, and many are beginning to recognise that the best time to learn is when everything is new and therefore important to the child.

Here is a series of five books designed to help parents to amuse, interest and at the same time to teach. *Shapes, Colours* and the Ladybird *a b c* each have their part to play in bringing the child to an early understanding of the reading process; *Counting* teaches him to recognise and understand the simple use of numbers, and *Telling the time* shows him how to relate the time on a clock face to his everyday life.

telling the time

by LYNNE BRADBURY

illustrated by MARTIN AITCHISON

Ladybird Books Loughborough

day-time
night-time

morning

afternoon

evening

It is 8 o'clock
in the morning.

Some people
are getting up.

Some people
are eating
their breakfast.

It is 9 o'clock.

Older children
go to school.

Younger children
stay at home.

SCHOOL

At 9 o'clock
Mummy is working,
Daddy is working.

It is 10 o'clock.

Everyone is busy.

What are they doing?

JIM
JILL

It is 11 o'clock.

The children are
having a drink.
Then they go out
to play.

At 11 o'clock grown-ups have a drink too.

It is 12 o'clock.

12 o'clock is the

end of the morning.

12 o'clock
is the middle
of the day.

At 12 o'clock
the children
are having
a meal.

Some are at home.

Some are at school.

It is 1 o'clock
in the afternoon.

Lots of people have a meal at 1 o'clock.

People eat different things.

It is 2 o'clock.

What are these children doing?

At 2 o'clock
the grown-ups
are busy too.

It is 3 o'clock.

Lots of people
like a cup of
tea at 3 o'clock.

It is 4 o'clock.

The children are coming home from school.

They are hungry.

STOP
CHILDREN

At 4 o'clock
the children
sometimes watch
television.

At 4 o'clock
on a fine day
they can play
outside.

It is 5 o'clock.

Mummy is busy.

She is cooking.

EGGS
PIE

It is 6 o'clock.

These people are going home from work.

bus stop

At 6 o'clock
Daddy is home.

BBC
NEWS
Daddy

It is 7 o'clock.

How do the children get ready for bedtime?

At 7 o'clock,
when the
children are
ready, it is
time for a story.

It is 8 o'clock.

The children are asleep.

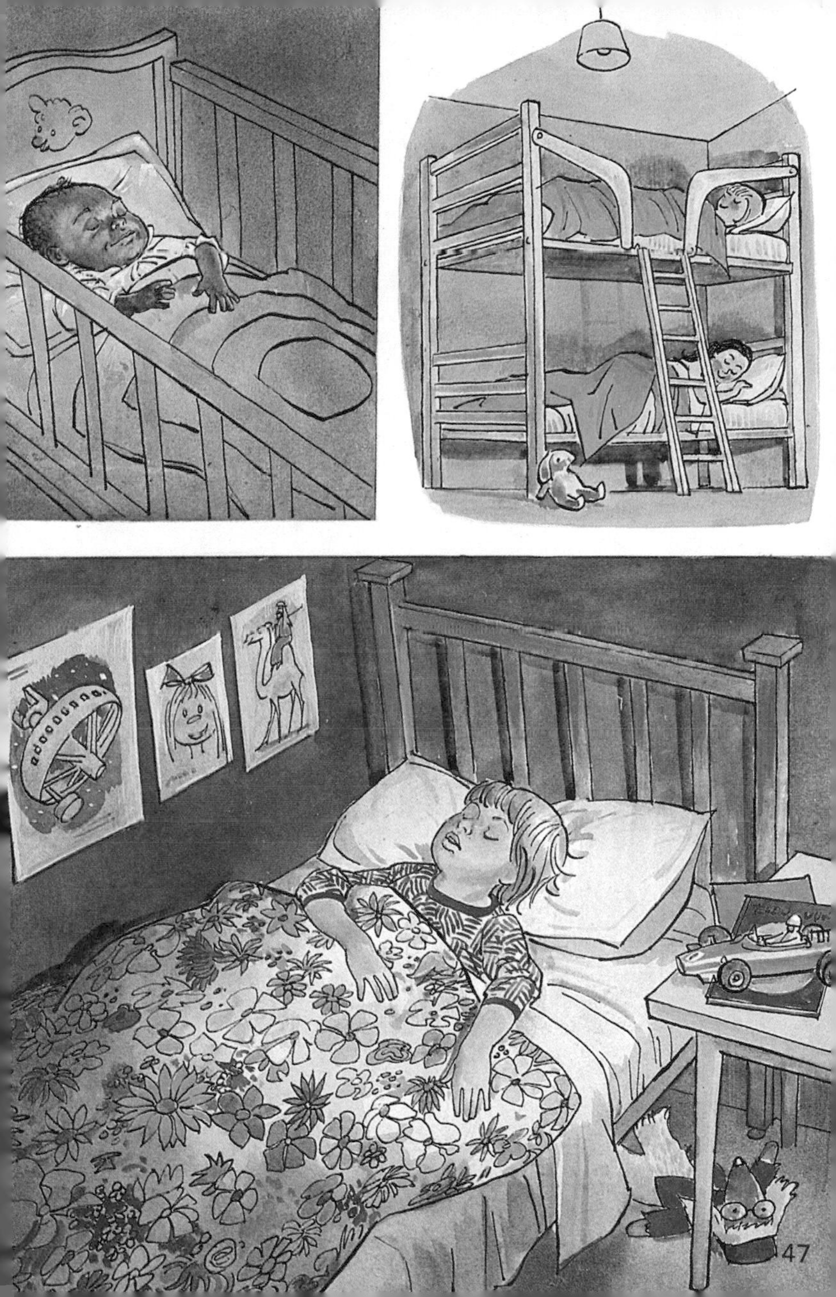

At 8 o'clock
Mummy is going out.
Daddy is watching
television.

ART
8 P.M.

half-past eight
half-past nine
half-past ten
half-past two
half-past three
half-past four

big hand

little hand

Cut out and stick onto card. Attach hands, using a paper fastener through the holes, with the big hand on top.